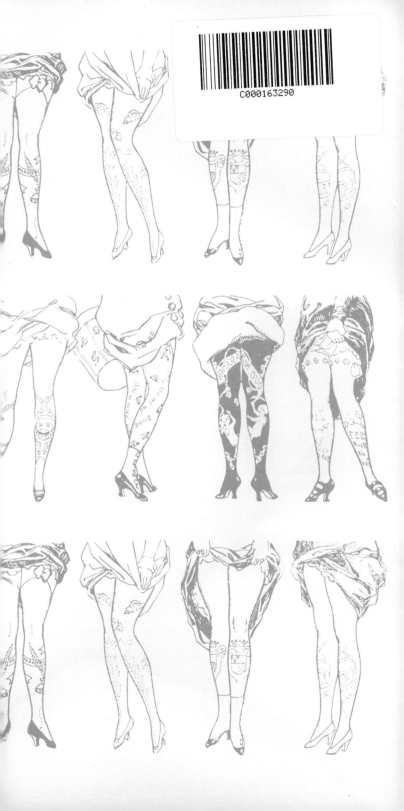

the
Stocking
Book

the Stocking Book

PAPADAKIS

Publisher's Note
The Stocking Book was originally conceived by Andreas Papadakis some
twenty-five years ago. He collected many images which he rediscovered
when he last moved house in 2006. The project was fully reignited when
his great friend Victor Arwas agreed to write the Introduction.

This book is dedicated to Andreas and Victor who are sadly not here
to see the book that embodies their great love and enjoyment of life and art.

First published in Great Britain in 2010 by Papadakis Publisher
An imprint of New Architecture Group Limited

PAPADAKIS

Kimber Studio, Winterbourne, Berkshire, RG20 8AN, UK

Tel. +44 (0) 1635 24 88 33
Fax. +44 (0) 1635 24 85 95
info@papadakis.net
www.papadakis.net

Publishing Director: Alexandra Papadakis
Editor, Researcher and Text: Sarah Roberts
Design Director: Aldo Sampieri

ISBN 978 1 906506 08 7

Printed and bound in China

Contents

INTRODUCTION by VICTOR ARWAS 11

STOCKINGS IN THE ANCIENT WORLD 13

DEVELOPMENT OF THE STOCKING 16

THE MODERN STOCKING 55

STOCKINGS ON THE RUNWAY 79

DESIGN AND DECORATION 79

CHRISTMAS STOCKINGS 115

ROYAL STOCKINGS 117

ETYMOLOGY 135

STOCKINGS ON THE SILVER SCREEN 135

STOCKINGS IN ART 151

BIBLIOGRAPHY & CREDITS 192

Introduction
by Victor Arwas

When a woman takes all her clothes off, she can be depicted as a pure, Classical nude. If, however, she keeps her stockings on, she suddenly becomes naked, an erotic creation capable of arousing the viewer's libido. This curious paradox has been observed and used by artists since the Middle Ages. Stockings range from extremely elaborate confections: multicoloured, embroidered, applied with sequins or precious stones, painted, striped or otherwise made into objects to be coveted, enabling the wearer to be desired.

They range from the shapeless utilitarian woollen stocking suddenly transformed by being black or allowed to droop erotically down the leg, to the breathtaking sheen of silk stockings drawn tight over the leg, held in place by an elaborate garter or garter-belt. Silk was eventually replaced by nylon or rayon, enlivened in certain decades by a central seam in the back of the leg (giving rise to the arousing gesture of straightening the seam), a tiny monogram or the variety of colours in the sheer quality of the transparent material, listed in deniers.

This book explores the astonishing variety of stockings from the eighteenth century to the present, the way great painters depicted them, the way illustrators and cartoonists made use of them, the way advertisements presented them, and the way they have developed, from practical woollen undergarments to luxurious silk creations, from the miraculous invention of nylon to the simple stocking hung from the mantelpiece waiting for Father Christmas.

12

History

STOCKINGS IN THE ANCIENT WORLD

The vibrant history of stockings and socks begins in the depths of prehistory. In their earliest incarnation, socks were probably little more than animal skins, tied around the feet to offer protection from the elements and rough terrain.

Garments resembling the modern stocking began to emerge in the period following the bloody Norman conquest of Britain in 1066. Norman fashion favoured the shortening of men's tunics to jackets, and breeches were eventually abandoned altogether. Women also wore stockings above the knee during this period.

These continued to be a highly popular mode of dress for several hundred years, becoming increasingly decorative and complex. The stockings were made by cutting woven fabric on the bias to permit some stretch, and the sole was applied separately. Decorative patterning, termed the 'clock', was added at the ankle to shape the stocking over the foot.

C'mon Babe

Why don't we
paint the town?

And all that jazz

I'm gonna rouge
my knees

And roll my
stockings down

And all that jazz

DEVELOPMENT OF
THE STOCKING

Knitting has been practised in the Arabic world since the first century AD, but the technique is not thought to have become widespread in Europe until the Crusades, beginning around 1095. The use of the technique to create knitted stockings, which retained a better shape and fit than their woven counterparts, did not become popular until the 16th century.

Initially, the production of knitted stockings was time consuming and labour intensive. However, the invention of the first knitting machine by the Reverend William Lee in 1589 allowed for much more efficient production of hosiery. Lee presented his invention to Queen Elizabeth I, who refused a patent on the basis that it would affect the hand knitting industry. Several years later Lee took his invention to France to present to Henry IV, but nothing materialised and Lee died in Paris around 1614 without fame or fortune.

After Lee's death, his brother returned to England with the design and began again without a patent. Steadily his business began to prosper. The machine could produce stockings from wool, cotton and silk, making them readily available across the social spectrum. Wool stockings were mostly worn by the lower class for their warmth, cotton was worn by the middle and upper classes, and silk was reserved for the wealthiest people and royalty. This is not to say that stockings did not have their detractors. In 1583, the pamphleteer Philip Stubbs published his *Anatomie of Abuses* in which he condemned the lascivious stocking:

"Their stockings in like manner are either of silk, Jarnsey, worsted, cruel, or at least of fine yarn thread or cloth as is possible to be had; yes, they are not ashamed to wear hose of all kinds of changeable colours, as green, red, white, russet, tawny, and else what not. These thin delicate hosen must be cunningly knit and curiously indented in every point with quirks, clocks, open seams, and everything else accordingly."

Whilst both men and women continued to wear silk, wool or cotton stockings and garters until the end of the 18th century, the emerging fashion for long trousers saw men abandon the stocking in favour of the sock. From this point forward, the stocking began to be considered exclusively as women's clothing.

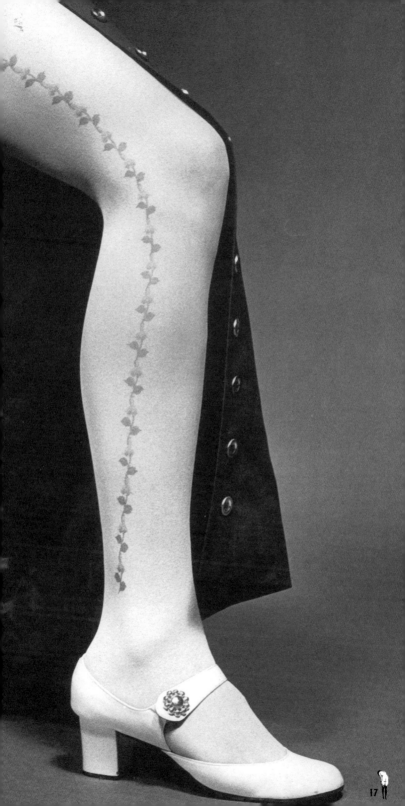

In 1864 William Cotton invented the first automated knitting machine, based on the design by the Reverend William Lee, which could produce a finer weave in the fabric. By the mid nineteenth century, a circular knitting machine was also available, allowing the production of seamless stockings. Seamless stockings were constructed of a knitted tube of fabric to which separate foot and toe pieces were attached. However, stockings made on circular knitting machines tended to bag at the knees and ankles, and so the design did not achieve mainstream popularity until much later.

References to women's hosiery were sparse throughout the Victorian era (1819-1901) as any public mention of women's legs was considered improper, and showing them was certainly indecent. Any glimpse of bare leg was enough to bring on a touch of the vapours, and even the sight of an ankle covered solely by a stocking was frowned upon in polite society. Stockings were generally black for daytime wear and white or coloured for the evening. They reached just above the knee and were held up by garters, although by the end of the century stocking suspenders were often sewn to the bottom of the corset. Striped and patterned stockings gained popularity in this period, as demonstrated in John Tenniel's illustrations for Lewis Carroll's *Through the Looking Glass* (1871), depicting young Alice in her black and white striped stockings.

Every

woman's

fortune

lies

between

her legs

– Balzac

·RAPHAEL·
·KIRCHNER·

25

The only sign of modesty in the present dress of the Ladies is the pink dye in their stockings, which makes their legs appear to blush for the total absence of petticoats.

The Chester Chronicle, 1803

Any glimpse of
bare leg was enough
to bring on a touch
of the vapours,

and even the sight of
an ankle covered solely by
a stocking was frowned
upon in polite society.

Garter, n.: An elastic band intended
to keep a woman from coming out of her stockings
and desolating the country.

—Ambrose Bierce 1850

Denier – The measured weight of the yarn. 5 denier is the sheerest and 100 denier is the most opaque.

Thigh Highs – Stockings that stay up on their own, without a garter belt. They normally have two or three silicone bands in the welt to help them stay up

Fully Fashioned Stockings – Knit to fit and do not stretch. They are manufactured flat and then seamed up the back. They can either have a Cuban heel (squared off at the top) or a French heel (pointed at the top). All fully fashioned stockings have a keyhole opening at the back.

Reinforced Heel and Toe (RHT) – This vintage-style hosiery has darkened, reinforced knitting on the heel and toe.

Any

public mention of

women's legs was

considered improper,

and showing them was

certainly indecent.

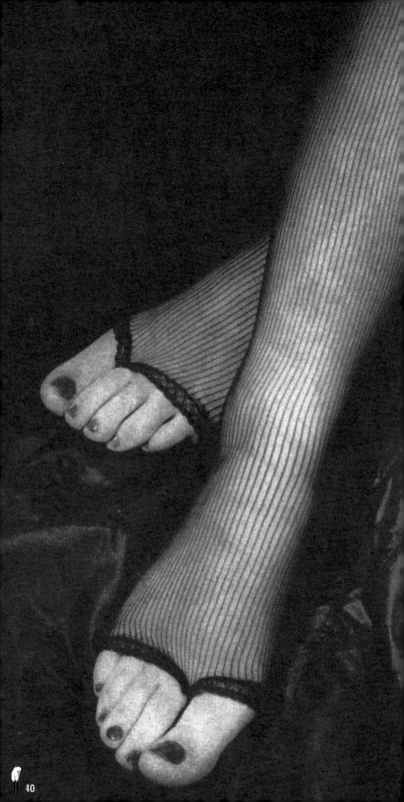

Mary Quant

47

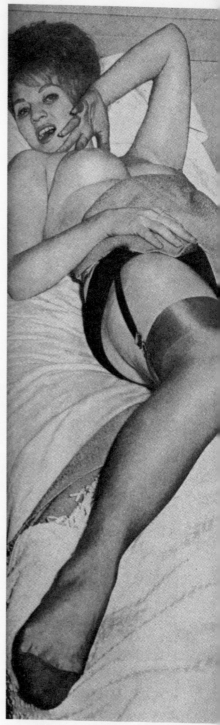

VOL. 2   NO. 4

French Frills

LA PUBLICATION
MAGNIFIQUE

**Eroticism is the
pornography of
the rich.**

THE MODERN STOCKING

After World War I (1914-1918) hemlines rose and long silk or rayon (known as artificial silk) stockings were worn again. As rayon stockings were very shiny, women sometimes used to powder their legs to dull them down. It is rumoured that women would often roll their stockings down to make it easier to dance, and rouge their knees to draw attention to the fact that they were on display, as in the lyrics of the 1975 song 'All That Jazz':

> C'mon babe
> Why don't we paint the town?
> And all that jazz
> I'm gonna rouge my knees
> And roll my stockings down
> And all that jazz
> …
> Oh, she's gonna shimmy till her garters break
> And all that jazz

During the 1920s, beige, skin coloured and pastel coloured stockings were in fashion, as well as patterned and embroidered stockings. Furthermore, feet, ankles and calves were on display, where previously they had been hidden by the black wool stockings worn by young ladies up until the end of World War I. During the Prohibition in America, ladies used to tuck hip flasks of alcohol into their garters.

In the 1930s, scientists at the DuPont company in the USA began experiments in molecular chemistry that would change the world of hosiery. In 1935 they discovered that by pulling a heated rod from a mixture of coal tar, water and alcohol they could create a filament that was strong, sheer and silk-like in appearance. This revolutionary new fibre became known as nylon, and it was first revealed to the world at the 1939 World's Fair, alongside the television set. It was advertised as "strong as steel" and "fine as a spider's web" and was initially used for fishing line and toothbrush bristles.

On 15th May 1940, the first nylon stockings appeared in New York stores. Over 72,000 pairs were sold on the first day alone and the Japanese silk market collapsed almost overnight. Over the course of the first year, 64 million pairs of nylon stockings were sold, quickly replacing the silk stockings women wore previously.

Photo: Peter W. Czernich

It is a widespread belief that the name 'nylon' is derived from the abbreviated NY of New York and the first three letters of London; however, there is no evidence for this. DuPont state that the name evolved from 'no-run' through several different incarnations to 'nilon' and finally 'nylon'.

During World War II (1939-1945) nylon stockings became scarce as factories instead had to focus on production of military tents and parachutes. Many women could not get hold of stockings, or could not afford them, and instead used leg makeup, gravy browning or weak tea to dye the skin, drawing a vertical line up the back of their legs to simulate the seam. American GIs could still get hold of nylon stockings, though, and they became the gift of seduction for British women. Some young women instead wore short ankle socks, but most returned to wearing stockings as soon as they were available again.

Throughout the 1940s and 1950s, women wore stockings fashioned to the shape of the leg. As nylon did not stretch, stockings had to be produced in many different sizes. They were knitted flat and then the two sides were joined manually with a fine seam up the back.

In the late 1950s, manufacturers discovered that they could add stretch to nylon by crimping it under heat. In 1959 DuPont invented Lycra, which is able to stretch up to seven times its original length without breaking and then return to its original shape. This new discovery dramatically improved the fit and comfort of stockings as well as their strength and durability.

Manufacturers continued to refine the design of William Cotton's nineteenth-century circular knitting machine, and seamless stockings with a reinforced heel and toe were introduced to the market. It took a while for these new stockings to catch on, as many women associated the lack of a seam with bare legs, still considered indecent, but they became increasingly accepted throughout the 1960s.

In 1959 tights were introduced to the market. With the advent of the fashionable miniskirt in the 1960s, attributed to Mary Quant, it was no longer feasible to wear stockings and many women instead opted for coloured and patterned tights. The convenience of not having to wear a girdle or suspender belt was a big attraction, and tights began

to fly off the shelves as iconic models such as Jean Shrimpton and Twiggy appeared in them.

Improved manufacturing and the use of spandex and elastane made tights a cheaper and more comfortable alternative to stockings, and by the 1970s sales of tights had overtaken those of stockings. Some influential models and actresses tried to set the trend for bare legs but it was not until the 1980s that it became completely respectable for ladies to abandon their stockings.

Tights remained popular throughout the 70s, 80s and early 90s, until 1995 when sales began to fall. This was attributed to the fashion for bare legs and changes in workplace dress code. By 2006 leggings and footless tights had become a more popular alternative, and stockings were largely relegated to the intimacy of the bedroom.

Nowadays there is a fantastically tempting range of stocking available for the modern woman (and even the modern man too). From bows to bells, lace to latex, fishnet to fence net, there are sexy stockings in plentiful supply.

64

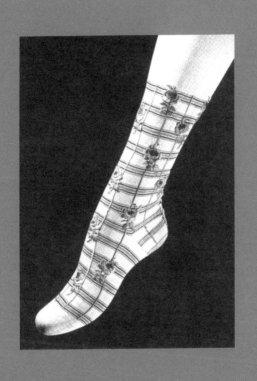

ℱrom

bows to bells,

lace to latex,

fishnet to fence net

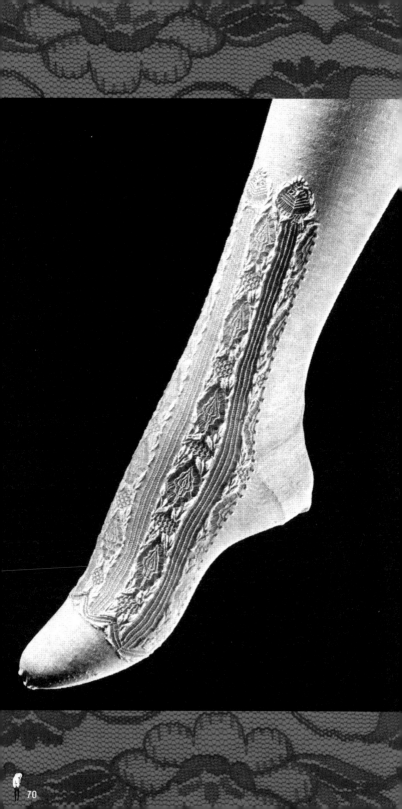

STOCKINGS ON THE RUNWAY

From London to Paris, Milan to New York, hosiery has made an appearance on the haute couture catwalk year after year. From the fishnets of the 1970s and 1980s to the neon shades of today, the fashion world continues its enduring love affair with stockings and tights. Even semi-transparent latex stockings have made it onto the runway thanks to Vivienne Westwood.

Though the fashion for bare legs dominated the catwalk in the late 1990s and early 2000s, by 2006 stockings began to appear on runways once again. In 2007 patterned tights made an appearance in white, black, silver and even tartan and animal print.

2009 saw lots of dark, deep colours that seemed to reflect the economic downturn: black, earthy grey, metallic silver, crimson, burgundy, deep orange, navy blue and teal as well as earthy brown, beige and cream. Though the credit crunch was perhaps best personified by the trend for laddered stockings and ripped tights.

In 2010, Jean Paul Gaultier caused a stir on the catwalk with his sexy stockings that had a motif of the Eiffel Tower running up the back of the leg. In the same year the celebrity trend for 'underwear as outerwear' made an appearance, with garters, suspender belts and lacy stocking tops ubiquitously on show.

DESIGN AND DECORATION

From scarlet reds to forest greens, pearly pinks to baby blues, snowy whites to classic black, stockings are available in a dazzling array of rainbow colours. From the utilitarian wool of the 1940s to the tantalizing sheer sheen of a nude stocking, today there is an endless choice of colours and patterns to suit every mood or occasion. Quirky designs from the 1980s include Mary Quant's gold tiger stockings, adorned with a shimmering tiger along the back leg, and even the signs of the zodiac. Today, the Scottish company Bebaroque offer a unique array of stockings with fringing, beads, crystals, sequins, bows, fans, ruffles, embroidery, pearls, lace, cord and wool embellishments.

Give me
just two
of your
vital statistics
and I'll
give you
tights
that fit

– Pierre Cardin

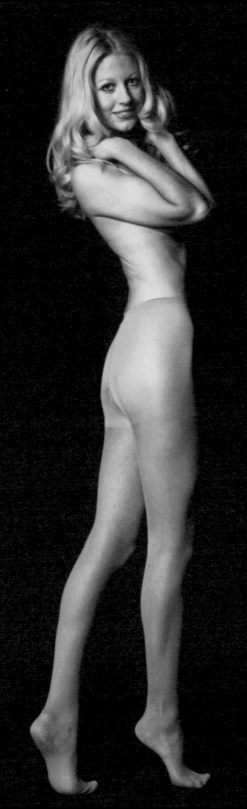

Too much practical lingerie
makes a dull woman.
An occasional frill is
good for the soul.

Vogue, 1932

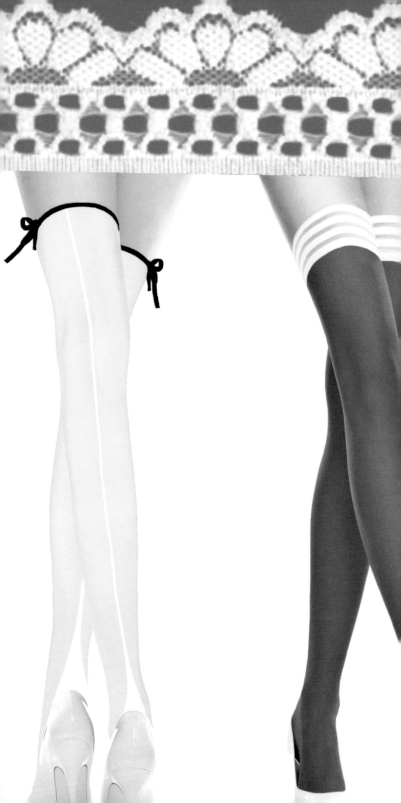

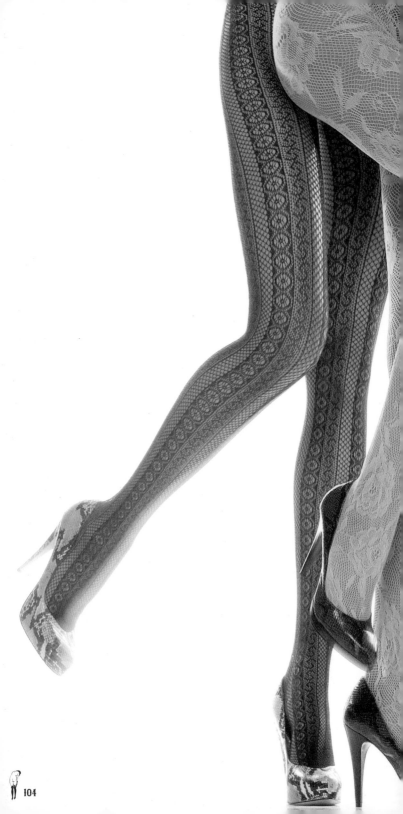

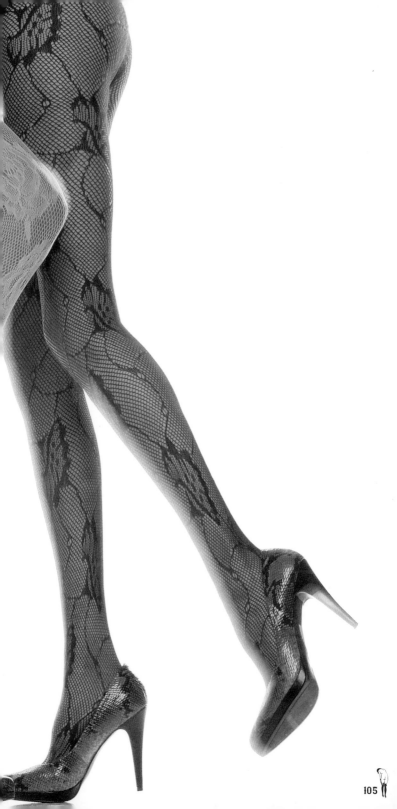

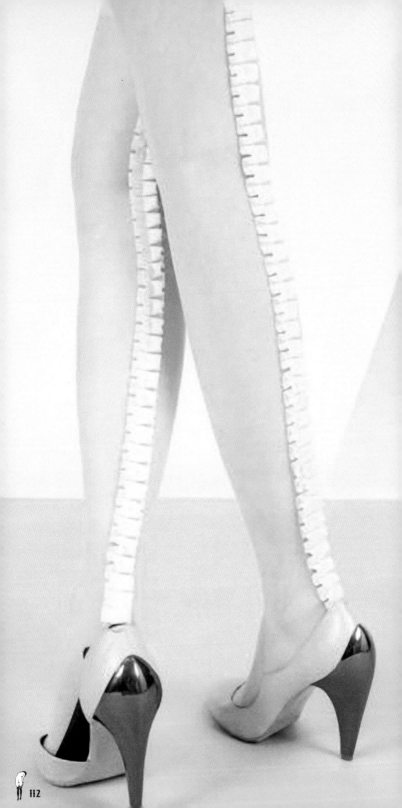

CHRISTMAS STOCKINGS

Christmas stockings are hung by the fireplace on Christmas Eve for Santa Claus to fill with treats and small gifts for children. There are several different tales that explain the origin of Christmas stockings, though none pinpoint exactly when the tradition started.

One story tells of a wealthy nobleman, living happily with his wife and three daughters. One day, the wife sadly passed away from an illness. Devastated by her premature death and having spent all his money trying to cure his wife, the nobleman was forced to move into a run-down cottage. Soon the time came for his daughters to marry but he could not afford their dowries, which caused him great anxiety.

St Nicholas was passing through the nobleman's village when he overheard the villagers talking about the unfortunate daughters. He wanted to help but knew that the nobleman would be too proud to accept charity. Instead, St Nicholas went to the nobleman's house after dark and dropped three bags of gold down the chimney.

The bags of gold fell into the daughters' stockings, which had been hung by the fireplace to dry overnight. When they awoke the next morning to discover the gold the daughters were overjoyed and were able to marry with generous dowries.

When the villagers heard the story they too began to hang stockings over their mantelpieces in the hope that St Nicholas would be equally kind to them.

Another theory is that Christmas stockings originate from a Dutch tradition. It is said that in the sixteenth century, children in Holland kept their clogs by the hearth, filled with straw for the reindeer. They also left a treat for 'Sinterklass' near the fireplace and in return he left gifts for the children. Over time, the clogs became stockings and Sinterklass became the Santa Claus we know today as the tradition spread to America and Europe.

A third theory is based on the Germanic figure of Odin. According to this theory, children would leave carrots, straw or sugar in their boots near the fireplace for Odin's flying horse Sleipnir. When Odin came, he would leave gifts or candy for the children in exchange for Sleipnir's food, to reward their generosity. It is claimed that this tradition survived even after the acceptance of Christianity in Belgium, Germany and the Netherlands, and the idea eventually became associated with St Nicholas.

ROYAL STOCKINGS

The first British monarch to wear silk stockings was Henry VIII, who wore purple and crimson designs specially made for him from silk taffeta. Sir Thomas Gresham, founder of the Royal Exchange and importer of stockings into England also made a gift of a "payre of long Spanish silke stockings" to Henry's son, Edward VI.

When Elizabeth I ascended the throne in 1558, knitting was already a widespread craft. She received her first pair of black silk-knit stockings from Mistress Montague as a New Year's gift in 1560, prompting her declaration that "I like silk stockings so well, because they are pleasant, fine and delicate, that henceforth I will wear no more cloth stockings". By 1588 carnation pink and many other colours were worn by Elizabeth. To protect her silk stockings from wear and perspiration she wore woven stockings underneath.

Records even describe the stockings that Mary Stuart, Queen of Scots, wore for her execution in 1586: "Jersey hose white under socks of worsted watchett (sea blue) clocked with solver, edged at the tops with silver; both knitted."

In France, around this period, Spain was also providing Henry IV's second wife Marie de Médicis with exquisite purple, red and orange silk stockings decorated with the French lilies or the Médici coat of arms.

Following this, Louis XIV's court set the trend for silk stockings along with breeches and brocaded coats. Louis XIV is depicted in several paintings wearing red, black and light blue or white silk stockings often adorned with bows or garters. Madame de Pompadour, the king's mistress, introduced the fashion for elaborate lace stockings.

MARS

Almost any young girl will confess
that her greatest weakness is for
the pretty things of the boudoir.

Vogue, 1916

A well formed nude
is never lost

– Willy

I guess

I'll have to find

A new,

a new kind

A guy who

digs my shiny

stockings, too

Those silk shiny stockings
That I wear when I'm with you

ETYMOLOGY

The word 'stocking' is derived from the Anglo-Saxon word *stoku* meaning 'sleeve', related to the word *stocc* meaning 'trunk' or 'log'. The earliest known usage of the word 'stocking' in English dates back to the 16th century.

STOCKINGS ON THE SILVER SCREEN

Despite iconic appearances of stockings in films such as *The Millionairess* (1960) and *The Graduate* (1967), the association of stockings and the silver screen has not always been a comfortable one. In 1930, Marlene Dietrich starred in *The Blue Angel* wearing a corset and black stockings. In response to the perceived risk of moral degradation, the Motion Picture Production Code was introduced in the United States; it expressly forbade nakedness, suggestive dancing and scenes of passion in film, effectively banning the on-screen appearance of the stocking.

During the First World War, actress Gaby Deslys attempted unsuccessfully to start a trend for bare legs, stating that she would cease to wear stockings until Germany surrendered to the allies. Similarly, in 1920, Hollywood actress Pola Negri went bare-legged, and in 1926 actress Joan Crawford stopped wearing stockings for evening wear. But despite the fact that actresses often led the way in women's fashion, the idea did not catch on – women found the idea shocking.

JOSEPH E. LEVINE presents
A MIKE NICHOLS-LAWRENCE TURMAN PRODUCTION
"THE GRADUATE" x
starring ANNE BANCROFT
and DUSTIN HOFFMAN . KATHERINE ROSS
Produced by   Directed by
LAWRENCE TURMAN   MIKE NICHOLS
Technicolor ®   Panavision ®   United Artists

I

Married

A

M:

Monster

From

Outer

Space

La mort aussi
peut être une source
d'inspiration
du strip tease

ELBEO

Supp-hose®
Panty

The ultimate support tights
for the fashion conscious woman

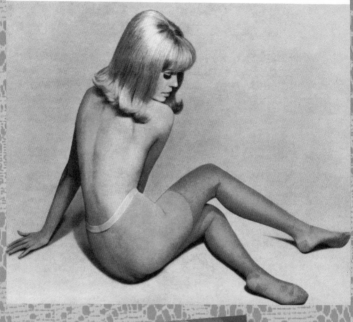

heer
LOUR
GHTS
by

lle

SHEER
THROUGH
N RESIST
  SIZE 1
40˝/102cm HIPS
  SIZE 2
9˝ TO 44˝
112cm HIPS

0% NYLON

E IN ENGLAND

e.65

DRIFTWOOD

SIZE 1

sheer soft
run resist

COLOUR
by

elle

RUN RESIST

SIZE 1 UP TO 40˝/102cm HIPS
SIZE 2 39˝ TO 44˝/99-112cm HIPS

S
H
E
E
R

C
O
L
O
U
R

by

elle

STOCKINGS IN ART

Around 1895, the act *Les Couchers d'Yvette* made striptease popular. Seen in Parisian shows, it consisted of a woman gradually stripping herself of her clothes in a futile search for a flea. The onset of 'striptease' led artists to paint women as if caught in the midst of putting on stockings. Even before this, artists showed a predilection for depicting women in stockings, as, for example, in Gustave Courbet's painting *Woman with White Stockings* painted circa 1861. Courbet's *Nude Woman Reclining*, believed to be lost for decades, was discovered in 2007. The painting depicts a sleeping woman with tousled hair, wearing white stockings and not much else.

Around 1907, Egon Schiele (1890-1918) began to produce erotic pieces of art, such as his paintings *Female Nude with Blue Stockings* and *Seated Woman with Green Stockings*. This overt depiction of female sexuality was met with widespread controversy.

Auguste Renoir (1841-1919), a key painter in the development of Impressionism in art, glorified in all forms of beauty, but particularly the sensuality of the female form with paintings such as *Girl with Red Stockings* (1886) and *Young Girl Slipping on her Stockings* (1895).

Henri de Toulouse-Lautrec (1864-1901) was another key figure in the art of 19th century Paris. Lautrec conveyed the nightlife of Paris in his paintings – its music halls, cabaret life and, of course, its brothels – witnessing the spectacle of Parisian life firsthand. Lautrec produced many of the posters and advertisements for the cabaret shows at the Moulin Rouge as well as paintings of the nightlife inside, where dancers performed the cancan to a keen audience. Beneath their skirts the dancers wore black stockings adorned with ruching and bows, and showed off their extravagant underwear.

Lautrec also focused on portraits of women in their stockings in paintings such as *Alone* (1896), where the black stockings of the model contrast with the light folds of her bedsheets, and *The Medical Inspection* (1894), which depicts two semi-naked women in white hues, drawing the viewer's attention to their black stockings.

Throughout the 1940s and 1950s the appearance of pin-up girls in magazines and on posters and postcards was very widespread. The artwork depicted beautiful, idealized women, frequently in their stockings, and the genre even gave rise to artists specializing in the field.

Mimi Pinson

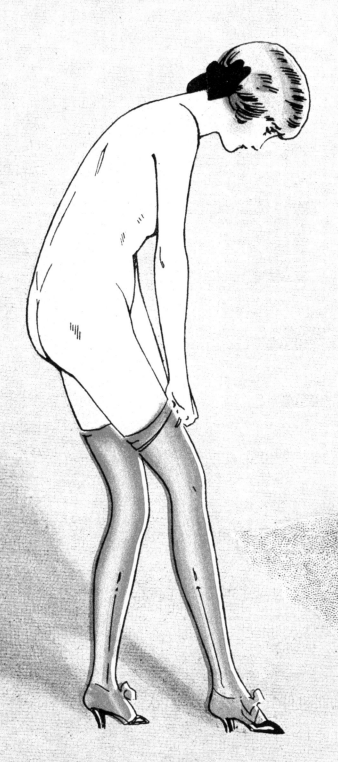

There are some
things which are hidden
in order to be shown off

– Montaigne

PRÉGER

DÉPOSÉ   PARIS

Ière MARQUE FRANÇAISE

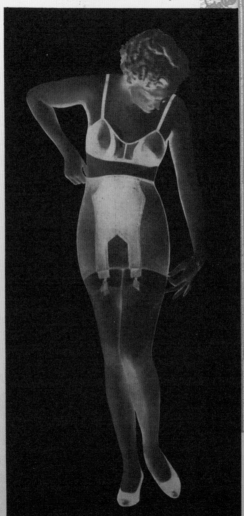

TULLEX

LA GAINE TULLE PERFECTIONNÉE

EN TULLE **DOGNIN**

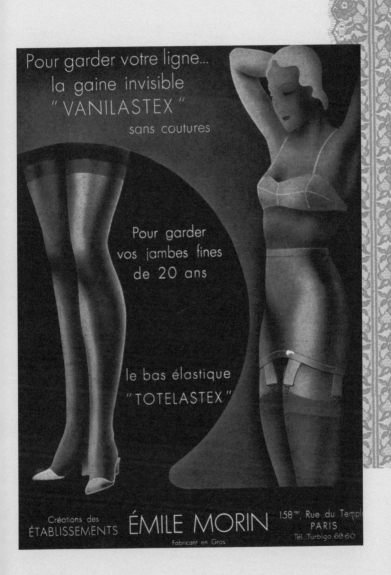

171

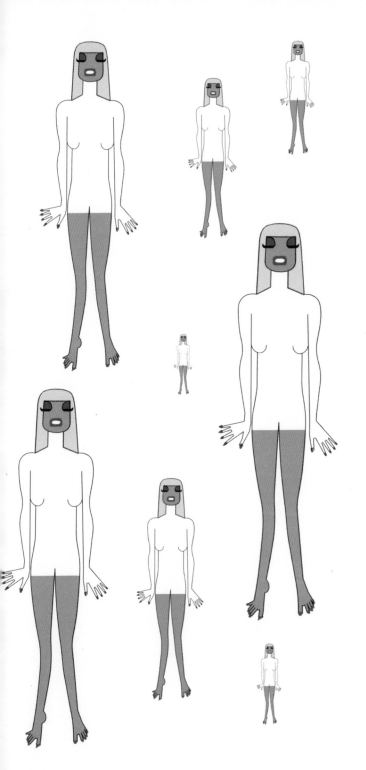

After World War II,
in Tulsa, USA, twice as many
women reported that they had
missed nylons than those who
said they had missed men.

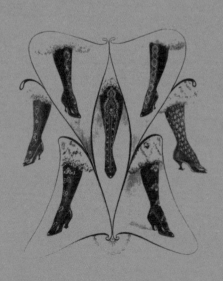

It has been suggested that the Eiffel Tower, built for the Universal Exhibition of 1899, represents a woman's leg clad in net stockings, with the four pillars representing the suspenders extending from the belt.

 I n olden days,

a glimpse of stocking

was looked on as

something shocking.

N ow heaven knows,

anything goes.

Anything Goes – Cole Porter

Do you know where

friendship ends

and passion does begin?

It's between the binding of

her stockings and her skin.

Stockings – Suzanna Vega

La gamm

C

répond à to

POUR LA
Bas "GUI" grisott

PO
Bas

BAS GUI , J

des bas

JI

es besoins

SPORT :
as " GUI " crêpe

tal

ES JOLIES

Yes, it's alright.

I said, yes it is, that's alright.

I may not want to admit it,

I'm just a fool for your stockings

I believe

A Fool For Your Stockings – ZZ Top

VALDES

Le haut du pavé

A. BAEHR

le bas
Hélios
BAS ET LINGERIE

Arwas, V., 2010. *La Vie Parisienne*. 1st ed. London: Papadakis.

Boucher, F., 1967. *A History of Costume in the West*. 1st ed. London: Thames & Hudson.

Broby-Johansen, R., 1968. *Body and Clothes: An Illustrated History of Costume*. 1st ed. London: Faber & Faber Ltd.

Chenoune, F., 1999. *Hidden Femininity: 20th Century Lingerie*. 1st ed. Paris: Editions Assouline.

Cunnington, P. & Willett, C., 1952. *The History of Underclothes*. 1st ed. London: Michael Joseph Ltd.

Day, J.A.C., 1975. *Decorative Silhouettes of the Twenties*. 1st ed. New York: Dover Publications, Inc.

Deutch, Y., 2002. *A Glimpse of Stocking: A Short History of Stockings*. 1st ed. London: Michael O'Mara Books Ltd.

Probert, C., 1981. *Lingerie in Vogue since 1910*. 1st ed. New York: Abbeville Press.

Rudofsky, B., 1947 *Are Clothes Modern?* 1st ed. Chicago: Paul Theobald.

Saint-Laurent, C., 1966. *The History of Ladies Underwear*. 1st ed. London: Michael Joseph Ltd.

Sternberg, J., 1972. *Kitsch*. 1st ed. London: Academy Editions Ltd. and New York: St. Martin's Press.

Sternberg, J. & Chapelot, P., 1974. *Pin Up*. 1st ed. London: Academy Editions Ltd. and New York: St. Martin's Press.

Sternberg, J. & Chapelot, P., 1971. *Un Siècle de Pin Up*. 1st ed. Paris: Éditions Planète.

www.stockingirl.com   www.stockingshq.com

Image Credits